GOAL DIGGER

BE A WOMAN IN BUSINESS NOT A WOMAN IN EVERYONE'S BUSINESS

BY

MARTHA VEGA

DISCLAIMER

The information presented in this book solely and fully represents the views of the author as of the date of publication. Any omission, or potential misrepresentation of, any peoples or companies is entirely unintentional. As a result, of changing information, conditions or contexts, this author reserves the right to alter content at their sole discretion impunity.

This book is for informational purposes only and while every attempt has been made to verify the information contained herein, the author assumes no responsibility for errors, inaccuracies, and omissions. Each person has unique needs and this book cannot take these individual differences into account. For ease of use, all links in this book are restricted through this link to facilitate any future changes and minimize dead links.

TABLE OF CONTENTS

INTRODUCTION

Thank you for downloading this fantastic guide—**"Goal Digger, Be A Woman In Business Not A Woman In Everyone's Business."**

I dedicate this book to my mother, Martha Alicia Vega, who raised 7 kids, started multiple businesses, was a top performer at several multi-level marketing companies all without speaking a word of English, she spoke a universal language, HUSTLE! That woman only saw opportunity, because that's what she chose to see. Gracias Mami.

The foundation to my life, Mi amor, Chris Thomas. You are the reason I've been able to achieve the unimaginable; your support and love has never failed me or our family...I love you.

Does your life seem harder than you imagined it to be? Do you dream of the day that you can live the life you dream of living? You know deep inside that it is the right life for you, but you are afraid?

You are not alone. So many people spend their lives waiting for the big break; i.e. like winning the lottery, or some long lost relative leaves them an inheritance so that they can live the life of their dreams, while figuring out what they were created to do.

If you will follow your passionate purpose it will be like stepping onto a track or path that has existed all along and all of a sudden door open and you meet the right people that can help you accomplish your passionate purpose.

They were always there, but you weren't on the path, so they were hidden from you. The financial capital to fund your work will show up in ways never imagined before. The blinders have come off and you are now able to see the opportunities.

Anyone can start a business in their spare time. The important thing when starting a business is to keep in mind that your goal is to be financially free. So, structure the business so that eventually it can run without you. Or maybe focus on using your company to build capital and then using that money to invest in other assets like positive cash flow property.

If you want to follow your dreams the easy way, then financial freedom is the first step. It removes the worry of having money and needing to work to put food on the table. It frees your time and your mind so you can focus whole heartily on your dreams and what you want to achieve.

If you have a dream that has been calling to you, now is the time to step up and say, "yes." Remember, "Fear knocked at the door, faith answered, and no one was there." When we get on the path of our passionate purpose, everything will fall into place, and you will have been guided to the right people and the provision.

Let's Bigin!

THERE ARE TWO TYPES OF WORK

Personal Development

It is not uncommon, for the terms, personal development, and growth, to be met with a certain amount of sighing and an expression of 'been there done that'. We've been learning about the idea since we were in school and we've been working on it since forever. So, what is going to be different about this one?

Whatever the subject, it needs to add value. Otherwise, trash it!. So, let's familiarize us with what goes into the whole process of personal development and growth.

Understanding Personal Development

1. It refers to the accumulation of life skills that help a person to live a productive and satisfying life.

2. PERSONAL Development and PERSONALITY Development are two very different things.

3. When we talk about personal development, we are primarily talking about achieving success. It could be professional or personal.

4. It involves setting attainable goals and using problem-solving strategies that will help you attain growth.

The very crucial point is, Personal development, unlike personality development, cannot be inculcated. It cannot be given to you in a beautifully wrapped gift basket or as a 4-week program! You are your only hope as far as personal development is concerned.

It is because it is a lifelong process. With every new hurdle, you will pick up a new skill and that skill will lead to more growth and development. Although there is no set path on how to achieve personal growth (since it is subjective)

Markers For Personal Development

❒ Improved Self-Awareness

You gain a better understanding of yourself. Your strength, weakness, abilities and also what is beyond your capabilities.

❒ Greater Self-Knowledge

It is one thing to be aware and an entirely different thing to know. When we undertake personal development, we have the opportunity to get to know ourselves better. Because the truth is, we know practically nothing about ourselves. Others learn more than we do! So, it is important that we find out more about ourselves.

❒ Learning New Skills

You will pick up new skills, related to your work or even to your personal life. There is an enhancement of our skill set, and we become proficient in more ways.

❐ Improving Existing Skills

It is not always about learning new things. Now and then, the armor which is already in the arsenal needs to be sharpened. You already learned so much over the years. Now, get on to making them better.

❐ Setting Better Targets

99% of the times, we fail to achieve our objectives because we set unrealistic ones. There is no shame in failing, but it is stupid to set a bar that is beyond one's imagination to reach. So, to develop, we must make it a habit of setting short term, achievable goals. For example: you want to lose weight, don't start an extreme 30 day challenge, start by eating healthy for 3-5 days(attainable goal)

❐ Identifying Potential

Remember, we can never be the best version of ourselves, until and unless we are doing what we love to do. You may also have some skills that you didn't know about! We'll be even better! Time to bring those to the forefront. Write a list of your top 3 passion drivers and grow them.

❐ Improving Social Skills

It is not only for the socially awkward. If you are someone who gets uncomfortable in social situations, then no doubt, personal development will help you to become more open and comfortable.

But also, people who are comfortable in social situations, the question is, "Are you interesting enough to spend time with?" Find out. Get to know everything about the person you are and compare it with the person you think you are. The results may just astound you.

☐ Personal Autonomy

In simple words, making a decision and executing it, without outside influence. You are the captain of your ship, and nobody knows how to sail it better than you. There is a sense of independence that comes from personal development. Write down your goals, and re-visit them daily, morning,noon and before bed.

People Development Must Be Your Best Investment

The right people training, development and also education, at the right time, provides big payoffs for you and increased productivity, knowledge, faithfulness, and share. Learn the approaches that will guarantee your training brings a return on your investment.

YOUR LIFE INFLUENCERS

Startup Advice: Advice From Experts To Start Your Own Business

Most entrepreneurs get paranoid over the idea of starting a business. With so many federal, state, and, local laws governing any business, it becomes crucial to make an informed decision about the venture. Here are a few steps worth considering before your business takes off in full swing.

❐ Initial Capital Investment

The very foundation of your business rests on the original capital amount you invest in it. Your funds initially could spell serious trouble for you in future. So, whether it's an online or an offline business venture, make sure that you're not low on the initial capital to be invested.

These days, local banks and microlenders have opened their doors for you to get loans for business ventures. As long as you have a healthy credit score, getting a small loan is simple.

Just keep in mind that you don't go overboard on your initial business expenses. Watch your financial moves carefully. Once your business takes off well and gets you a huge profit, you could consider taking another loan to scale the company.

Experience In Managing The Business

❐ Expert Business Plan

Having concrete business guidelines is imperative. Most often, it's observed that home-based and other small-scale businesses fail poorly due to a lack of business "blueprint." Such businesses suffer substantial monetary losses. Without a concrete business proposal, almost 70% of the businesses wind up within a year of being established. Therefore, a rough draft of the business plan taking into account all the minute details are necessary for any business venture.

The business plan should explicitly define the target audience for your products. It should also present a detailed description of the average cost per product and your expected profit on each product. Besides, it should also portray the desired break-even point and your expected income from the business. Thus, for a smooth sailing business, it's imperative that your business plan defines the ways of converting your business into a cash generating system.

Take Valuable Guidance From A Business Mentor

The most successful people you see and read about are made up collectively by mentors in that industry, for example; Steve Jobs to Marc Benioff, the top CRM software, Salesforce.com

Don't hesitate to learn from the experiences of your most admired business mentor(s). Find someone who is doing or did what you plan to do and learn from their mistakes and successes. Any time I started a new job i would go to the top performers to learn from them. Do the same. They will show you the right way to expand your small-scale business into a vast business empire. Never miss out on an opportunity to gather those pearls of wisdom from an established businessperson.

Keeping in mind all the factors as mentioned above you can ensure a long life for your start up business enterprise.

Hang Out With Winners And You Will Become One

Given this reality, it becomes paramount to discipline our ways of thinking toward the positive and productive. The mind is like a muscle, and flexing it can be difficult at first, but given some time and exercise, positive thought can become second nature.

Meditation, or simply making a daily ritual of affirming your goals to yourself can be excellent starting points on this evolution. There are, of course, more complicated steps. However, those are bridges you will want to cross when you get to them. My seven-step program, referred to at the bottom of this book covers those advanced techniques in detail. Now that we've established the need to affirm your principles of action and personal goals let's take a look at some of the most important of those principles.

❒ Abundance Is A Function Of Natural Law

In nature's laws of cause and effect lies the universal truth that abundance is always present in our world, needing only to be claimed by those willing to initiate their cause. Act as if you're already that person you imagine yourself to be, best Real estate agent, top producer, best speaker...you get the picture.

❒ Net Worth Begins With Self Worth

In any free market transaction, the correct value must be demonstrated to attain rewards. Therefore, one must create superior worth and directly associate that value with every action he or she takes. Because all people will inevitably act to their benefit first and foremost, you must respond in kind by elevating your value to a level of superior market worth.

❒ With Freedom Comes Responsibility

Having personal freedom means, above all, that you are given a choice of whether to act as master of your destiny or be acted upon haphazardly by those who are looking out for their best interests. To be truly prosperous. However, one must be willing to live by right principles.

For some, it goes without saying, but one of these can easily be summed up by the Golden Rule. Positive goals can never be accomplished with any lasting result through harm or deceit. But the most profound implication of this pillar is that YOU DO have the ability to live abundantly whenever you so choose.

❏ Intent Manifests As Reality

In this principle, has been referred to by various scholars and luminaries by such names as "The Law of Attraction," "The Principle of Manifest Intent," and even "The Power of Prayer."

It is simply the act of making your will known to the universe, and contributing the necessary effort to bring that will about. Because this principle is so far reaching and powerful, it becomes paramount to discipline one's thoughts toward the positive.

❏ You Are Your Best Asset

Don't ever stop learning, always look for ways to improve yourself. Whatever that may mean for you. For example reading books that's relevant to your goals, finding a mentor in your industry, taking a dance class or a workshop.

❏ Your Life Has Profound Impact

Reaching even beyond the infinite value of your life, you can gain tremendous significance, simply by remembering those whose lives you sincerely desire to change for the better. Your loved ones, children, friends, and colleagues will all benefit tremendously from the positive actions YOU take.

❏ Money Is Granted Value By Transactions

Because the amount of money you make is always directly proportionate to the value that you bring to the table, your value is legitimized by profit. If sufficient value is not present, no transaction can be performed. This principle serves to protect and benefit both parties.

❏ Success Is The New Normal

As Rupert Murdoch, one of America's greatest moguls has said, "The world is changing fast." No longer is it reasonable for prosperity to remain exclusive to the select few of society's elite. One need only watches the evening news to see fast acting and energetic individuals making leaps and bounds every day toward leveling the playing field of American business.

❏ Ownership Equals Freedom

True freedom is only possible through independence. As long as one must rely on an outside source for survival, he or she is not free. As Alexander Hamilton said, "Power over a man's subsistence amounts to the power of his will."

GET TO WORK, NOW

How To Replace Bad Habits With Good Ones

You probably know something about the influence of habits in your life. However, you may not realize how strongly they affect you until you try to change them. Don't worry. You're not alone if you struggle to quit a bad habit or establish a good one. In this section we'll explore the three factors that create habits and three powerful strategies to replace your bad ones with good ones.

Noted psychologist William James once noted that, "We are mere bundles of habits." From the time, you wake up in the morning until you go to bed at night, you'll run through an astonishing number of habitual routines.

Unless you stop to notice that, you probably won't, because these routines have become subconscious and automatic. They go unnoticed because you don't have to pay attention to them. Habitual routines are a great way to save energy and efficiently get stuff done.

Your habits may be cued, or triggered, by the time of day, your location, what you are feeling, what you are doing, and who you are with.

For example, some habits (like brushing your teeth, taking a shower, getting dressed, drinking coffee, eating breakfast, and kissing family members good-bye) are triggered when you wake up to get you ready for the day ahead.

Some habits are triggered when you arrive at school, work, or the gym. Some are triggered by inner sensations such as hunger, thirst, boredom, fatigue, sadness, loneliness, or excitement. Others are triggered by being with specific people or doing specific activities. Habits can be triggered by some combination of any or all of these cues

According to the most current research on habits, there are three factors that create a habit: the cues that trigger it, the behavioral routine that responds to that cue, and the reward that the behavior seeks to bring you. Together these form the habitual loops that repeat automatically whenever the appropriate cues are triggered.

If you have bad habits that you want to quit, it's important to understand what cues you to automatically engage in that behavior. It's also helpful to know what reward you are seeking from it. If you are trying to create a new good habit, it's important to know how to support that habit by consciously cuing and rewarding the behavior you desire.

So, how can you apply this knowledge to either quit an old habit or establish a new one?

If you want to quit a habit, you can begin by understanding what reward you are seeking from the behavior you're engaged in. For example, are you smoking for the chemical or oral stimulation, the social interaction, or for a break from sitting at your desk?

If you can get a handle on what is driving your habit, you may be able to find a substitute activity that will give you the same reward, without the negative side-effects. The goal is to put a new behavior in the middle of your familiar cues and rewards. Substitution can be a really successful strategy.

For example, when you are cued by location, time, activity, inner feeling, or other people to engage in your "smoking behavior," you could substitute chewing gum, taking a walk with friends or co-workers, or drinking green tea in place of smoking. You can experiment with what behavior can give you the reward you're seeking without the negative consequences you want to avoid.

New Behavior And Habit

If you have a new behavior that you want to make into a habit, see if you can insert it into a familiar routine. For example, you could insert meditation into your waking-up routine, your lunch-time routine, or your going-to-bed routine.

You could insert working out into your getting-the-day-started routine by putting your workout clothes next to your bed; or into your driving-home-from-work routine by putting your gym bag in the front seat of your car and visiting the gym on the way home.

If you can tie your new behavior to cues that are already in place and other activities that you already do, you're more likely to be successful.

If you're still having trouble getting started, see if you can anticipate the reward you want from your new behavior and imagine how good that will feel. This is a great strategy to get yourself over that initial hump of inertia. I use that one all the time to get me started on my workouts.

One more important insight about creating new habits: certain habits have tremendous power to positively affect other habits in other areas of your life. These are called "keystone habits." When you establish a keystone habit, you'll notice that you are more deliberate, intentional, and successful in everything else you do. Establishing a keystone habit is another potent strategy.

One of the most amazing keystone habits is meditation. When you insert even a short meditation into your waking-up routine, you'll discover that not only do you feel better to start the day, but you do everything more consciously. You become more relaxed and present in whatever you're doing.

As a result, you are much more effective and enjoy it all the more. Meditation builds inner skills that supercharge the other changes you'd like to make in your life.

Creating Good Habits - The Fundamental Building Block In Internet Business Success

The fundamental building blocks of success in internet business is all based on creating good habits habits that are goal-oriented and based on the goals you want to accomplish and the things you want to achieve in your life.

Here are five important steps which will help you to understand what a habit really is, how to set up a plan to help you create good habits, how to be consistent and deliberate in setting your habits up, and how to move on to the next habit once one has been accomplished.

❏ Awareness And Will Power To Create A New Habit

Understanding that trying to have more discipline will not help you in forming a new habit. Neither will trying to change all your bad habits right away or trying to form a new habit overnight.

Be aware that the above mentioned are myths when it comes to creating new habits, what you really need is a good bit of will power so that you can harness it towards forming new habits.

When you become aware that something you are doing is not in line with what you really want to accomplish, that is a good motivation to immediately begin forming a new habit.

❏ Create A Ritual

A ritual is different from a habit in that a ritual is a very important part of your life, it's imagining the actual behavior and what it's going to look like. A ritual has a trigger, which is a specific thing that happens or a specific action that gets taken to signal it's now time to start the ritual.

An example of this might be to start exercising (which is the habit). The ritual is the behavior that would get you there with the help of a trigger. An example of a trigger would be the alarm clock going off at a certain time to help you in the ritual of getting up, or the placement of your workout clothes could be a trigger to remind you it's now time to begin your ritual of getting dressed for your workout.

A ritual is a very deliberate thing because you are planning out in detail the behavior you plan to do on a consistent basis.

❏ Inevitability Thinking

Inevitability thinking is putting things into place to make it inevitable that you will do that particular thing and making sure it will happen without any distractions getting in the way.

Going back to the example of exercise, it could be putting the exercise clothes on right way to keep yourself from being distracted or placing an object such as a water bottle somewhere where you will run into it and it will remind you that you need to drink your water.

You could even tell a friend that if you don't follow through, you'll buy something for them (maybe a dinner) which would be a good motivation to make sure the action you are wanting to take is inevitable or else you would have to follow through as promised. Another example could be a reward that you give yourself when the task is completed ensuring that it will get completed because you really want to receive that reward.

Inevitability thinking is planting incentives or setting reminders to help you get to your goal, to help remove the temptations for you to easily get distracted. Putting these types of mechanisms into place when you become serious about forming a new habit will help keep you from getting distracted from many things that would keep you from habit-forming success.

☐ Be Consistent

It is scientifically proven that mental or emotional "muscle memory" occurs when an action is performed over and over consistently. The performance being perfect is not as important as making sure that your action is happening over and over on a consistent basis. It's easy to rationalize in your mind many excuses to not be consistent, but if you can make a deliberate choice it will pay off in the end.

Resistance towards being consistent is natural, as humans we naturally resist change. It doesn't mean you are not disciplined, that you don't have enough will power, or that you are not good enough it just means you need to stick to it longer and eventually it will become a habit and you'll begin to reach your goals. Consistent effort over time will yield desired results.

☐ Start The Next Habit

You will have a good sense when your efforts of creating a new habit have paid off, and now your habit is a habit. If success is reached one habit at a time, then keep plugging away at creating new ones - one at a time. Create a list of habits you wish to start and prioritize them in the order that you need to accomplish them. Imagine how many new habits you can create in a year if every three to four weeks you are working on a new habit.

Some examples of good habits in internet business that you could form would be: using a timer to track your time worked on certain projects to help you stay focused, writing new content for a blog just a little every day, spend two hours a day working on just your internet business.

Ask yourself at the beginning of the day what it the most crucial thing to your business that you could accomplish today that if it got done you'd be really happy, or maybe you could just block off free times on your schedule so that you don't overload yourself with work.

Start with the habit you want to work on now, follow the steps as outlined above and you will be on your way to creating habits that stick and in turn help your internet business take off in a successful way.

Start Your Day With A Personal Success Ritual In 4 Easy Steps

Every person should have a morning success ritual. People that have morning success rituals are more productive, happier and healthier.

First, you want to wake up a little bit early, because your ritual will be around 90 minutes long.

Step 1: When you wake up, first thing you need to do is drink a half liter of water. This is even before you brush your teeth. Your body is dehydrated in the morning so you need that water to start a productive day.

Step 2: Now is the time to work out a little. It`s better to exercise in the morning, because it increases your heart rate, and you will have much more energy during the day. Try to exercise for about 30 minutes. If you exercise later in the day you will feel tired and your productivity level will drop.

Step 3: After your workout, you should eat breakfast. Think about the food you eat in the morning. There is a reason why breakfast is the most important meal of the day. You have to eat rich nutritious food in the morning so you will feel better and have more energy. Your breakfast should include whole grains, low fat protein, low fat dairy and fruits.

Step 4: After breakfast,try to meditate.

You don`t need to learn advanced meditation techniques. Just close your eyes and focus on your breathing.

HOW TO TURN YOUR STRUGGLE INTO SUCCESS

The Secret of The Millionaire Mind

Everybody wants to know the secret of the millionaire mind, but they'd be surprised to learn that everyone has it. It's just a matter of wiping away all the road blocks that are preventing it from surfacing and doing its thing.

Have you ever heard the expression, "You are what you think?" It means that if you think positively, you will enjoy positive results, but if you think negatively your results will be negative.

We might tend to think that the 'secret' is something special that makes people productive, but it's not. It stems from having self-esteem and confidence, which goes toward making you an active person.

Active people, for some reason, tend to make good decisions that get them to their goal. Whether we are negative or positive, it will show in how we think through a situation.

Let's take a simple goal like mowing the lawn. Let's suppose you've never cut a lawn before and don't know the first thing about it. What do you do?

First, you'll look out and realize it needs cutting. A cynical person would just sit back and say, "I don't know how to do that," whereas an active person would think, "I have to learn how to do that or else the property will look terrible."

The difference between the positive and the negative person is that the positive person doesn't just look at the problem. He or she sees it as something that requires learning a skill and getting it done.

The secret of the millionaire mind is to focus on the goal, rather than on the problem. It is possible when real thought rules. Those of us with a positive attitude get things done, one way or another. We have the self-confidence and the courage to move forward, to learn new things, to apply what we learn.

A millionaire mind doesn't take no for an answer. At every obstacle, it continually seeks solutions. Plans are made and put into action. Persistence and determination go hand in hand to create the desired success.

Knowing how to set goals and make real plans to achieve them is crucial. Having self-esteem plays a role here because, without it, we doubt our abilities. In this frame of mind, we set unachievable goals to reinforce our beliefs that we are incapable (or unworthy) of becoming rich. Or worse, we just don't set any goals at all.

To recap, the secret of the millionaire mind covers several areas that we can all master.

❏ Build a positive attitude and healthy self-esteem

❏ Be determined and confident

❒ Develop the habit of looking at the solutions, rather than at the problems

❒ Develop good goal-setting skills and an effective plan to make them happen.

Facing the fear and doing something about it to change your life around takes courage - but everyone can do it. By understanding what is stopping you from moving forward is the first step to tapping into the secrets of the millionaire mind.

Once you know what it is, you can face it. By having a strategy of your own to keep you focused will give you something to hold onto when you start doubting yourself and your abilities. Some people create vision boards or a journal, and some even put little notes up around the home or their desk at work.

Whatever you can think of to remind you to stay on track, it all helps to keep you focused on your goal whether it is becoming a millionaire or creating a systemized business where your time isn't required.

Leverage Your Strengths

There are things we do so well and effortlessly that we often forget we are good at them. We call these things strengths, talents, or gifts. A 360-feedback report identifies highest scores as seen by others.

However, the participant needs to interpret what his or her real strengths are. Participants in a 360 should review the strengths that are apparent in their 360 reports and ask:

- ☐ Have these powers played out in my career thus far? How?

- ☐ Am I continually using these strengths in my career and personal life?

- ☐ What would happen if I were to utilize these strengths more regularly & fully?

- ☐ Why Build on Strengths?

- ☐ It is our Strengths that lead to real success in our careers, NOT lack of weaknesses.

- ☐ Strengths may come naturally to us, often from an early age.

- ☐ Others tend to overlook our weaknesses if they respect our strengths

In the absence of different data, people will assume Strengths: "She is exquisite in this area; therefore, she must be good at everything else."

Strengths can create the Halo Effect, meaning that a positive perception is quickly reinforced.

Remember, goal setting and action planning should first focus on strengths and then on those weaknesses that will impede success.

Develop Your Strengths

Develop Your Strengths Knowing your strengths provides a sound basis for building for the future. They are the best basis on which you can build. You need to recognize your strengths, grow your strengths, observe your strengths and look at your muscles.

Strengths are not just what we perceive about ourselves but how others understand about the particular qualities we bring and hold.

While our strengths are necessary there is a danger that you're not accurately aware of your strengths and talents. Often as people grow, they become experts in describing their weaknesses and spend time trying to address these faults rather than building on their strengths.

As a result, some of their strengths can lay dormant and ignored, as a consequence, these strengths are undeveloped and anthropic overtime. However, when you are acutely aware of your strengths and confident in them, you can do things that you might have been much more hesitant about in the past. As you use your powers, you become ever more confident in their value and application.

Recognize Your Strength

Recognize Your Strengths A good starting point is to articulate what you think your strengths are. You can supplement this by honestly summarizing what you think other key people, such as your family, colleagues, and the boss would regard as your strengths. Looking at your strengths through different perspectives alerts you to begin to see yourself as others see you.

At one level, you can do this by imagining yourself standing in other people's shoes and commenting on your strengths. Another approach is to ask people directly what they perceived as your strengths, or to request a colleague or coach to ask them on your behalf.

You might be able to use a kind of 360° written feedback tool that many organizations have available for their staff. It can help to write a list covering

- ☐ What do you think your five key strengths?

- ☐ What do you think your colleagues would see as your five key strengths?

- ☐ What would your close family members or friends think be your five key strengths?

Growing Your Strengths, Your strengths never stand still. You are either growing them or if you allow them to stagnate they will be declining in effectiveness. As you look back, you can often see how your strengths have been changing.

You can identify the strengths that have been consistently a valuable part of your assets and those that you have adapted and grown as a consequence of circumstances and experiences.

Developing your strengths is all about making what is good even better. You need to understand how you would identify strengths that need nurturing and growing.

TURNING IDEAS INTO PROFITS

Entrepreneur Profit - How To Turn Your Ideas Into Profit

Being an entrepreneur, you are subject to a fiercely competitive market. You will, however, wonder how an entrepreneur benefit when the competition is very severe. It is the secret of some brilliant entrepreneurs which is 'hobby.'

Hobbies usually stimulate one to formulate brilliant ideas, which can then easily be turned into something quite profitable. You just need to be guided on the details and then you can start working on it. Ideas can be very intriguing because, with the passing of time, they sometimes turn into big dreams.

One great example of this is writer's. Their passion for writing, if put to good use, can quickly turn into something profitable. You can apply your writing skills in article and site content writing, product and website content reviews, content re-writing, press release writing, E-book writing, advertising copywriting, and so on and so forth.

Business experts say that the number of successful entrepreneurs is forever growing. It is because they are doing what they love most and not what they are compelled to do.

Their common goal is to transform social issues into a productive entrepreneurial activity. Their ideas prove to be long-term solutions to social problems that cripple a nation.

A mere perception, when rightfully nurtured, tends to expand into more productive and qualitative output. It does not benefit the entrepreneur alone but the end-user as well.

Turning Your Passion Into Profits

The key to happiness and fulfillment in life is the discovery of a major definite purpose. Your goal is tied to your pursuit, value, self-worth, personal direction and achievement. Value is always maximized when the object is discovered. Either you are living your purpose, or you are living off of your fears and insecurity.

Remember there are no securities; what you have is opportunities. Building your life around your dreams offers the best chance to maximize your talents and gifts. That's how to benefit yourself and the world instead of blending with the crowd.

By definition, your passion is love in motion. Your passion is a meshwork of your pass-time, hobby, inborn talents, experiences, a particular skill, failures, success, learning or training. Don't be surprised that failure and bitter experiences are included in the definition of passion.

Experience is learning from your mistakes and wisdom is not repeating the same mistakes. Yes, other people want to benefit from your knowledge and expertise, too. What we hear often is the success stories, but you must know that failure is the back door to success.

By the way, know that there is market or niche to every idea. Yes, your riches are in your niches. You just have to define, confine and find your niche. It is called target marketing.

How do you then turn your passion into profit that can benefit you and others? Here is the four cardinal process you can use as a rough guide to turning your passion into profit:

Passion–>Prospects–>Pre-Sell–>Profits (Monetization)

Start with your passion by providing quality content. All of us are value shoppers to some extent. "Don't try to be a woman of success; be a woman of value," says Albert Einstein. Don't make the mistake of starting with money. Nobody starts with the end-goal! You can package or repackage your passion in a different format: course, eBook, physical book, report, manuals, seminars, workshops, mentorship programs, home study courses. Just to name a few especially if you are an information marketer.

Then quality content (value) will attract prospects or potential customers. Initially, these are called prospects. When your information solves the prospects' problems or meets their goal or aspiration, they are pre-sold to you already. It is how these people become your audience or subscribers to your idea or perspective on issues.

Potential customers are already pre-sold. People buy into you before they buy your products. In other words, you make friends before you make sales. We know that people love to give their money to people they know, love and respect.

It is even more powerful when you position yourself as an expert your unique selling proposition. Always know the reason why people are coming to you. Take a stand, and it is a numbers game, and there is no money in the middle.

The last step at the beginning of the end of the sales process is monetization. It is a fancy way of saying that the prospects who are already pre-sold in their minds have now become paying customers. They have used their hard-earned dollars to purchase your products, good or services. Here, they are no longer prospects but customers.

You must follow-up because there is the back-end and relationship must continue into the future. It is the way to make more money and minimize refunds with excellent customer service.

Ways To Turn Your Passions Into Profits

1. If you read books, then you can probably write your books. It is not hard to start an e-book business for example. Otherwise, you can send your manuscript to various publishers offline.

2. Start your blog. It is more than possible to share your passions on a blog and to get a massive following. It can be

monetized as well as you can offer training or books etc. to tempt your fans to invest in you. Check out some of your favorite blogs to get ideas as to how they monetize their work. For example, you can have banners on your blog, or links to affiliate offers that you trust, etc.

3. Start an e-store. eCommerce, eBay, and Amazon are huge these days. People love to have the convenience of shopping online. You can start a store by companies by searching Google to find the best platforms. Many of them provide all of the training needed but if you are not that techy then think of investing in a coach to assist you.

4. Create a membership site. If we look at a dating site, for example, think about how you can make a monthly income by having a place where people are looking for love. Love will never go out of fashion, so this may be a great area or niche market to get into. There are many other areas that you can create a membership site in though so don't be put off by thinking that dating sites are the only option.

5. Start a franchise. The great thing about a franchise is that the business model is already set up so as long as you have the leverage to get started, you can get a piece of the pie. It is hard work though as you may need to be hands on or at least be involved more than doing something online.

6. Online product promotion. It is my favorite option as one can promote anything to anyone and this means fantastic commissions. You are selling virtually, so there is no need

for physical products unless you want to sell tvs and such like. You can take your passions and become an affiliate for anything relating to what you choose. TIP: Sometimes the best commissions are small, not well-known niches.

These are just a fraction of ways to turn your passions into profits. Start researching other people that are already doing what you may want to do and see how they are doing it.

Strategies To Increase Your Income

Find a coach or mentor and expand your network. One of the quickest ways to increase your income is to change the people with whom you spend the majority of your time. It is often said that if you take the median income of the people with whom you spend the majority of your day, that number will serve as an accurate predictor of your income.

Forming mentoring relationships and networking with individuals who have achieved a higher level of financial success will expand your knowledge and expose you to new investment ideas and unprecedented opportunities to build wealth.

Get paid what you are worth. If you are an employee, that means going after higher-paying jobs in your industry. If you are a business owner, that means going after larger clients and deals.

It is important to make sure your time is directly aligned to where the lion's share of your income either is or is going to be and to make sure that you are doing the most important activities every day that will change the condition of your life or business financially.

How To Increase Your Income - Marketing Advice

Increasing income comes down to four main functions which are closely connected:

❒ Create Demand For Your Products

Improve your marketing functions get bright ideas on how to build more demand for your services or products. Improve your internet presence, your brochures and company image. Open new lines of communication with your public, such as surveying them to find out what is desired.

❒ Promote Yourself

Get out there to let people know who you are. Make phone calls, YES pick up the phone people! Send letters, join referral groups, be active in the community, and get your face known. For the best effects, make sure you're dressing well and smiling. If you do that, people will think, "Hey, I like that person." And we all like doing business with people we like.

❒ Sell Your Products

How well do you close the person who responded to your marketing? You can market all you want, but if you don't close, you aren't going to get paid. Look for ways to improve your sales process: take a course in sales techniques, attend seminars, or visit a library and read up on sales books.

❏ Improve the quality and delivery of your product

You also need to make sure that your products live up to people's expectations. If you don't have a good product, you won't survive very long. Look for ways to improve the quality of your product and how efficiently you deliver it to your customers.

All of this may seem outside of what you'd expect from a financial advisor, but if you think about it, it shouldn't be. People come to get advice on how to improve their financial condition, and increasing their income is the most important thing they can do.

And if an advisor can help them look at their business and make it grow, that will help them achieve their goals all the more quickly.

ACCELERATED SUCCESS

Bootstrapping Entrepreneurs - How Do You Create A Business That Works For You Instead of You For It?

Unless you want to create another day job for yourself, where you are a slave to the customer's wants, read on to find out more.

To create the perfect business, you should follow this small list of guidelines that will help you develop your business where you are not really in the day-to-day equation (after setting it up of course).

It does not mean that you will not have to do any work or that it will be easy. Any business worth its salt takes a ton of work to set up and get right. However, once you set a business up the right way, you can operate it on autopilot and move on to other money-making opportunities.

Here is the short list that you should use as a template for when you are setting up a business:

1. Are the selling and the money collecting automated without any human involvement (i.e. there needs to be credit card processing, a sales letter, and small human requirements)?

2. Is the shipping either digital or automated through a third party? If you have to hand ship anything in your business,

then you are working in the business. You want to be on the beach or laying in your yard in a hammock. Leave the packing and the shipping to the people that work for a living.

3. Can you walk away from your business for weeks to months at a time? You need to make sure that your business does not require your day to day involvement to keep it running. If it is very customer service oriented, you may want to think twice.

4. Is the customer service outsourced? It can be done later as you get a huge clientele, but in the beginning, you will at least want to organize your business in a way that you can outsource customer service later.

If you can get all 4 of these steps into your business design, then you are well on your way to becoming a hands-off entrepreneur instead of working in your business. One of the perfect types of businesses that fit this model is the information product business. Information products are sold on-line all over the world 24hrs a day, almost entirely on autopilot while you do the things you enjoy.

Pros & Cons of Discovering A System That Works For You 24-7

Have you ever thought about having a business in the form of a system that can run itself automatically? Sounds too good to be true, right?

Are you familiar with a system that works for you 24/7 on autopilot?

There is, however, a few "Pros & Cons" to this business which I will cover shortly so that you may decide if you would like to benefit from having your own business from home utilizing this system or choose not to too.

❒ The Cons Are

1. You have to after discovering this system, set aside the time to go through the tutorial videos and follow the step by step set up poses.

2. You have to attend webinar training at least once a week to be educated on how to utilize the system properly and learn how to use various marketing strategies so that you become successful in making an income on autopilot.

3. After the system is up and running, you have to be prepared to set aside about 3 hours per day to do marketing online using what you have learned in the webinar training.

You have to set aside this time especially if you start out as somebody like me when I first discovered the system and did not know anything about it before my discovery of it. You cannot drive a car unless you have learned how to use the controls first.

Example: How to steer, where the brake pedal is, accelerator, clutch, indicator lever and then how to be able to put all that you have learned into practice actually to be able to drive and develop your driving skills.

❐ The Pros Are

1. No risk trial period of using the system.

2. Free training on setting up the system, utilizing the system and training provided in various marketing strategies that show you step by step how to put money in your pocket.

3. Multiple income streams built into the system in the form of affiliate programs paying you affiliate commissions that you receive on a daily basis 24/7.

Build The Business of Your Dreams -Tips To The Perfect Business

Most people who start their own business do so because they wish to have more freedom. And while a successful business can result in financial freedom, many times the business owner becomes a slave to the firm, working 24-7. But there's no real freedom in that.

To build a business that gives you freedom to do what you want, when you want - in addition to financial freedom - follow these tips:

1. When building your business, create ways that do NOT require you to work one-on-one with clients or customers. In other words, develop passive sources of income.

This way, you won't be trading time for dollars. You'll be creating wealth from your knowledge, experience, and expertise. You may choose to work one-on-one with a few customers or clients, but they'll pay handsomely for this privilege.

2. Don't try to do everything yourself. Build a team of players who can keep the business running smoothly even when you're not around.

3. Create systems for everything. If every part of your business is systematized, you won't have to be around to make sure things are running smoothly. Everything will be delegated to members of your team or outsourced to other individuals or businesses.

People And Systems - They Power Your Success

If you want to turn things around in your business or take it to new heights, it pays to put more effort in these two areas. They are the key to sustainable growth and a business that is not entirely dependent on you.

Think about your own business. What likely got you to the first $500,000 wasn't enough to get you to $1M unless you made some changes along the way. With so much at stake - more time, money, control and freedom - do they get the level of attention they should? Here are a few things to consider:

When hiring employees or subcontractors, do you have clear goals and written expectations and standards?

Are routine tasks for each employee documented for easy training and development?

Does your company deliver what you promise customers each and every time?

When someone is out or leaves, can others jump in without difficulty, so customer care and other critical tasks are performed with the same level of quality and success?

Do your people look for ways to improve customer satisfaction or other areas of the business or view that as your job?

Could you go on vacation for two weeks without worrying or always calling in?

Whether you depend on employees, subcontractors, vendors or partners, the right people are a necessity for most business owners. And if you want those people to be the best they can be, to develop and stick around, you need systems in place to help them.

❏ Where To Start?

As an established business owner, you likely have an existing team and relationships, so let's start here. Make a list of all your employees, subcontractors, vendors/suppliers and partners.

❏ Employees

Are they a good fit for your business today and moving forward? What skill gaps exist for individuals or your team as a whole. Can these be addressed with training? Is your team open to change and new ways of doing things? With technology, today, this is sometimes an area that needs addressing. Does each employee have a current job description with clear responsibilities and expectations? Have individual and business goals been developed, shared and mutually agreed upon?

Sub-Contractors, Vendors & Partners

Do you have the right ones for your business? Is your business too dependent on any one provider, leaving you vulnerable? Are their standards the same as yours? Do you evaluate options periodically to understand pricing and assist in negotiations (even if you plan to stay with current providers)? Have expectations been mutually agreed upon and in writing where appropriate?

While loyalty to people is often a strength in small businesses, it can be a weakness if you are quick to hire and slow to fire. It's not easy to let go of relationships; you probably view many of them as extended family. But if you are honest with yourself, this can be a powerful exercise - and one that can make a big difference in customer service, growth, and long-term profit!

That's why systems are so important. With documented systems, people know what to do and how to do it. It makes training easier and more efficient. New employees can hit the ground running and start to contribute quickly.

Systems also make it easier for all employees to take on new responsibilities or help out others without difficulty.

Talk about a great development tool. Equally important, it takes away the stress when someone calls out sick, goes on vacation or leaves to take another job. To get the most out of your people, make sure you build levels of authority into your systems as appropriate.

Levels of power are simply decision-making tools - so individuals can handle customer issues, close sales, resolve problems and keep the business running! It eliminates the need for everything to go through you the owner and gives your people a sense of empowerment to do their job.

H.O.P.E.S THE FIVE RULES TO RICHES

Help

Rule number one is to start thinking in a more giving way."We make a living by what we get, but we make a life by what we give." - Winston Churchill If you want certain people to give you tips and business leads start by giving them something of value. Don't just walk up to them and ask them to teach you everything they know.

You need to develop a good relationship with potential clients. After that, they will be more than happy to share any tips or leads without you even asking.

Opportunity

Golden rule number two is to set a plan of action and stick with it. Since we all seem to make up excuses about why they have not started this or that yet, we lose our momentum. I'll start this tomorrow or maybe next week until we never bother to get around to it. You must set a time and date to accomplish something and stay focused on it.

Power

Number three on how to become productive is to follow the right people and learn from a life mentor. Follow someone who has success. Study their habits and learn what they did to become rich. Don't just listen to just anybody.

Take action and invest on what you have learned. Knowledge is not power, it is potential power, and it is useless if you do not apply it to your goal. You must invest in something to give you a chance to succeed.

Effort

Making an effort for ourselves is a positive way of improving our confidence and self-belief. Setting the responsibility of looking after ourselves, how we look, how we spend our time, getting the most out of our work, our relationships all indicate a person who feels that their life is meaningful. That person will not settle, They are prepared to make the most of each day.

Systems

Sometimes in entrepreneurship, when sales start to fall and income drops, we start looking for magic keys and secrets to solve the problem. Unfortunately, seeking secrets (that usually don't exist anyway) takes away from your business and ignores the knowledge and assets you do have. While it is important to continue your education by learning new things, when your business is down it can be faster to work with what you've got.

When the going gets tough, go back to basics and refocus their efforts on actions that bring's results. The fastest way to do that is to use what you already have such as your products and services, and existing customer base.

Understanding Money Velocity In Your Business

Understanding money velocity can be a very beneficial to any entrepreneur or business person. If you are an entrepreneur or just want to make some extra money- then listen up because this will help you tremendously.

☐ So What Is Money Velocity?

The velocity of money is just a measurement or an equation that will tell you how fast you are recouping your money. For example, If you put $20 into advertising, then how long would it take you to get that $20 back?

It is assuming that you are getting it back at all (of course). So, money velocity is the actuality of how fast the money is moving. This idea applies to business as well as investments. If you are looking to invest money into a business or an investment, then you will want to know the velocity of the return on your investment.

So let's take our example from before and say that you are looking to invest $20 into advertising.

A big question you should be asking yourself is " How fast am I going to get my $20 back?"

If you have a somewhat automated business, then the velocity of money will be much easier to figure out. If you were to look at any investments, it would also be being a relevant question to ask how fast your money will return to you.

THAN THERE'S YOU

Real Entrepreneurship Is Focused On Creating Positive Cash Flow

Business is not a business, and you are not an entrepreneur until and unless you are generating positive cash flow. Cash flow is king. It is the lifeblood of every business. The business people we respect are the ones who have lifted themselves up to success through sheer hard work, determination, and strategy.

They are the people who couldn't get "seed funding" or "capital injections," the ones that had to be smart and savvy to make ends meet and find ways to generate income from the start. They are the real entrepreneurs.

The real entrepreneurs are still using their initiative to manage risk and generate a profit, but their focus is on acquiring or creating cash flows not on creating unlimited business plans that look good on paper but deliver nothing of value in the real world.

In an era of easy money and get rich quick schemes we have forgotten one of the golden rules of successful entrepreneurship; create something that people want and are willing pay for.

What is the point of being in debt if the business you own or the assets you own don't produce an income that is greater than the money needed to service the debt? In business, we sometimes talk about the size of the entity as a means of avoiding the issue of cash flow and profit.

It is the positive cash flow that makes these equity investments viable because they generate money instead of spending money. A real entrepreneur is not interested in "paper profits" or inherent value they are seeking positive cash flow which can be used to buy additional wealth creating assets or re-invest in the business.

Business is only viable, and genuinely wealth is creating if it makes more than it spends and generates cash flow for growth and investment. It is the cash flow that feeds the business, allows it to prosper so that the business can eventually be sold and its value realized.

If you're a business owner, seek out every possible way to reduce your expenses, increase your sales and improve your ability to generate not just one, but many cash flow positions. It is what the most successful business people do to become wealthy.

They create or acquire 'cash flows' for a future sale or exit. If you own assets, ensure they are positively geared and that you are generating and receiving positive cash flow[s] at all times. The future success of your enterprise depends upon it.

Understanding Value

❒ What Is The Value?

Value is the key to profit. Understanding value can tell you a lot about how to generate greater benefits in any business.

Profit is the difference between your costs and the price you get for something - anything - in the marketplace.

Your Available Alternatives Define Value

In other words, where there is an available substitute for anything - goods or services - most customers will value them about the same. It is one reason why banks tend to offer very similar interest rates, and airlines tend to offer very similar fares. If you don't see a difference between two options, why would you pay more for one than another?

It is precisely where competition comes in. When you do something easy that creates value, a competitor can do the very same thing - and might do it for a nickel less just to get the customer. The limit to most competitors' willingness to cut price is almost always defined by cost. It means that most competitors will reduce their prices to take customers away from you up to the point where they start losing money on the deal.

CONCLUSION

With your mission, your vision and your goals now more clearly mapped out, the next thing to do is to start following that blueprint **H.O.P.E.S** to make your goals happen.

And this begins by recognizing what will support your goals and what isn't helping you to get any closer to them. Too many of us work incredibly hard thinking that we're getting closer to our aims when we're just moving further and further away from them. We're just procrastinating.

At one time, you had hopes, dreams, and plans for a great future. But circumstances, events and the trials of life, have caused you to put your plans on hold.

But, a little while has become a long time. So, you figured, why bother. It's too late for anything to come of it anyway.

Whether it is in business or everyday life, determination and motivation are key factors in obtaining goals of any kind. The determination is overcoming challenges. Whenever an obstacle gets in your way, you will find a way around it.

Motivation is the reason behind your determination. What is the reason for starting your business? Is the reason respect, independence or self-esteem? These are all great motivators.

Don't give up on your dreams. If you give up on your dreams, then you give up on yourself. Don't do this. You can do it. It takes the effort to imagine. If it is worth the effort to believe it, then, it is worth the effort to live it. Go, realize your dream.